A Man if West Destiny

An Arrangement of Words

by
Gerome Mauricio

© Copyright 2025 Gerome Mauricio

ISBN: 978-1629673028

All rights reserved. No part of this book may be reproduced in any form or by any electronic or mechanical means, including information storage and retrieval systems, without written permission from the author, except in the case of a reviewer, who may quote brief passages embodied in critical articles or in a review.

Trademarked names may appear throughout this book. Rather than use a trademark symbol with every occurrence of a trademarked name, names are used in an editorial fashion, with no intention of infringement of the respective owner's trademark.

The information in this book is distributed on an "as is" basis, without warranty. Although every precaution has been taken in the preparation of this work, neither the author nor the publisher shall have any liability to any person or entity with respect to any loss or damage caused or alleged to be caused directly or indirectly by the information contained in this book.

This is a work of fiction. Names, characters, places, and incidents either are the product of the author's imagination or are used fictitiously, and any resemblance to actual persons, living or dead, events, or locales is entirely coincidental.

v25-0430

Dedication

To my mother Sandra.

Because you have endured
so much in this life.

Thank you.

"…Seek first to understand, then to be understood."

~ Stephen R. Covey

"Life imitates art far more than art imitates life."

~ Oscar Wilde

Oh, how the world can unravel with the smallest of phrase
Some words punish some or are novel to others in so many ways

Table of Contents

Preface .... *xiii*
Thinking of You *19*
Where The 101 Continues… *69*
   1 - A Gift's Responsibility 72
   2 - Creative Righting 73
   3 - Greetings Carte Blanche 74
   4 - Please, Nothing Personal 75
   5 - Dear Georgia [O'Keeffe] Obsession Some 76
   6 - A Patriot's Hill 77
   7 - I'm Migrant 78
   8 - The Tortas and the Hair 79
   9 - Just Ice 80
   10 - LBD 81
   11 - Hands Around the World United 82
   12 - First Impressions 83
   13 - Finders Keepers 84
   14 - 'dence Audition 85
   15 - Governing Omnipotent Deity 86
   16 - Passage 87
   17 - No, Child Left Behind 88
   18 - Against the Wind 89
   19 - Lips Serve Us 90
   20 - A Tree Plainly 91
   21 - Add Diction 92
   22 - Strangers in the Night 93
   23 - Body Shamed 94
   24 - A Simple Man's Redemption 95
   25 - Saved By The Bell 96
   26 - Two Heads Better Than One 97
   27 - K-no-w Love Lost 98
   28 - Three GOATs Gruff 99
   29 - Dinner Date 100
   30 - One Nightstand 101
   31 - A Special Moment's Remissness 102

32 - Not Even Close	103
33 - Three Little Words	104
34 - REFUSE	105
35 - The Mad Had-Her	106
36 - The Mythical "O"	107
37 - Downtown Abby	108
38 - The Gem in Eyes	109
39 - Since Ability	110
40 - Over That Hill	111
41 - Betwixt	112
42 - The KIND	113
43 - Letting Go	115
44 - A Fatal Attraction	116
45 - When Opportunity Knocks	117
46 - Broken Windows	118
47 - The Mind Over Matters	119
48 - A Pathetic Point of Hugh	120
49 - That Loving Feeling	121
50 - Love Letters	122
51 - Keep Dreamin'	123
52 - Writer's Block	124
53 - Master Key	125
54 - Empty Nest Syndrome	126
55 - The Time of Day	127
56 - "S"talking	128
57 - The Two Ring Test	129
58 - Dirty Dozen	130
59 - Another Riddle	131
60 - A Unicorn Pickle	132
61 - UNCHaiNED	133
62 - Crying Wolf	134
63 - Mettle Fatigue	135
64 - Love Is	136
65 - One's Ick of Ant Behavior	137
66 - Eye Scream	138
67 - What It Takes	139
68 - Red Her Ring Remains	140

69 - There Once was a Lady 141
70 - Err of Familiarity 142
71 - A Tell of a Tail 143
72 - Sweet Sedate 144
73 - Only Cooks 145
74 - None Prophet 146
75 - Never In Off 147
76 - Bear BnB 148
77 - 9-5 149
78 - Baaad Times 150
79 - Returning Grace to Jenna's Side 151
80 - Bygones 152
81 - Dark Where It's Deep 153
82 - Huff and Puff 154
83 - Mourning Coffee 155
84 - Aural Pleasure 156
85 - Serf n' Turf 157
86 - Use It or Lose It 158
87 - A-muse-ing 159
88 - Happiness Eases Lonely People 160
89 - A Two Ring Test 161
90 - Everything Nice 162
91 - Skin Trade 163
92 - A Spice Most Requested 164
93 - Clever Girl 165
94 - Socialist Security 166
95 - Designated Reconnaissance Of Nearby Environments 167
96 - A Man's Grown Opinion 168
97 - The Tipping Point 169
98 - Give a F--- 170
99 - Monkey See Monkey Do 171
100 - A Beautiful Lesson 172
101 - RnR, No R and R 173
Keep It Simple Stupid 175

Preface

Hello, and welcome to the thing I've done. I'm assuming you are a mature audience. This collection comes in two parts. The first ranges from, let's say, some form of poetic lyrics to lyrical poetry; not quite poems. Inspired by interacting with just one young lady. The second is a series of flash fiction short stories all inspired by 101-word fiction while living along the U.S. 101 Freeway in Ventura County, California.

Born and raised in South Carolina, I spoke gibberish until the age of five. My twin brother being my translator from the language we created for ourselves. I began writing before speaking coherently; passing love notes to girls. I required speech therapists and began my journey playing catch up in language and communication, due to a confusion of the world around me. My parents divorced and soon after my little sister was born. I grew up in Texas even more confused. I excelled in math and reading though I was still years behind in social awareness and maturity, awkwardly trying to follow; still not understanding of understanding writing, nor was I encouraged to do so.

I moved to California after high school to build a relationship with my father. I was soon on my own, completely trying to figure things out. However far behind I was in 'how the world works' no longer mattered, for I then I received a rude awakening. I tried to learn from my reactions, my failed actions, and the actions of others while slowly starting to write as therapy. A (now-permanent) work injury left me jobless and homeless; requiring me to rebuild myself.

Attempts in relationships and flings led to lots of alcohol and drugs. A lot of regret and misunderstanding. A lot of enlightening and beautiful moments as well. Then I met V; never did I consider what was to happen. I, 26(M). She, 21(F). We worked in a restaurant alongside each other, each day for about two years. We built the kind of relationship that two separately unavailable people will create before the opportunity arises, and they cross paths emotionally. I understand that she's not here to defend herself. We were sarcastic and tongue-in-cheek with each other; making fun of each other, then holding and dancing. That's when things progressed. That's when I let my guard down. 2008. It all started by giving her a few words:

> Thinking of you
> Thinking of you with a smile
> Thinking of you makes me smile
> Thinking of ways to make you smile
> Refusing those that don't

Then a kiss. I started chronicling our ups and downs, back and forth, in a way I knew how. I was in unfamiliar territory. The cocky confident man got hit with reality. Things can turn in one moment. One choice can make her not feel safe. We apologized for how we treated each other. I tried and tried to make up for my mistake. She'd leave and come back. Repeat. Then gone. Only fear, jealousy, and anger were present. So much anger in myself for letting myself be affected. There were attachment and abandonment issues that I didn't realize I had. Having no one and nowhere to turn to, I felt the need to escape back into hallucinogens and more. Anger lessening. Writing more. That's when I finished the book of "poetry" for V's birthday. {So poorly put together} A kind of farewell. A kind of justification and validation, irrationally sought by me, that what we had did happen. There was also a letter I included where I wished her the best and goodbye. It was hopeful, cheery, de facto. Too personal to include here. I've looked back and feel a bit cruel for giving her the book but know the need to have done so is who I was.

Shortly thereafter, I stumbled upon a short story contest in the local news magazine. Published my first year in attempt, I continued to write. The second year is when I created Miss Ahjanee (misogyny), a pseudonym for the type of story I wrote. I thought "Please, Nothing Personal" was funny. Over the next few years of the contest Miss Ahjanee would continue to be published. I was onto something. I knew I was better at understanding writing. I started to author other stories under Aaron Knout (airing out; as in dirty laundry), though he was never published. More attempts in relationships and flings showed a pattern that I've come to understand more about myself and others. Writing somewhat. I was told by people that, "I shouldn't be here." while others said, "Don't go there." I found myself somewhere between neither here nor there. Sometimes feeling that the only things I knew were the things that can't be taught. Certain that our choice in each moment creates our beautifully wonderful path to tomorrow. Understanding that actions make it so that sticks and stones may break some bones, but help words develop futures. My search for a meaning resulted in something quite average.

With no contest, I focused on work and other things. A book was nowhere in my reach. It was more of a lifetime goal. I was so alone and isolated during Covid, my ability to write had disappeared I thought. Fast forward to summer of 2024. I came to a revelation and wrote more than sixty stories as I challenged myself to write a story a day. That brings us to now: the culmination of my approach on life's 'wonders.' I still require more understanding in writing but understand more my abilities when I do write. I was just going to publish my stories. More thought urged me to include the "poetry" to help you get a feel for the emotional progression and mental attitudes of one to write such stories.

    It is my intent for you to read the book front to back. In the first part, I hope you can realize a soul lost in desperation, trying to find the light in his brilliance. Then for the second part, I've placed the stories in an order for a particular feel throughout your reading. If a picture is worth 1000 words, then what do you get for 101 words? There are virtually no names in this book. The characters are not related. There have been several 'hers' over the years. Remember, these are fictional stories. Within, you will come across adult topics, the many ways we may interact with ourselves and others, and the many ways we may commit misogyny daily. I do not consider myself to be any more of a misogynist than the next, but I don't get to judge that, you do. I just try to bring some things to light for further understanding, for further discussion. Once we know our limits, then we can tend to its prevention and maintenance as needed. Yet, there are several misogynistic aspects not covered. Perhaps for another book. Perhaps another person's stories. For now, some simple words from an even simpler man:

From my heart to my hands
the magic has been broken.
But if I can then you can
with the words that I've spoken.
Yet somehow someway
Something's still lost from
my head to my lips,
but what I have found
I will happily give…

Thinking of You

Under the Influence of Life, Love, Loss, and Drugs

Thinking of You

Seeing you is a reminder of how I've somehow failed. I knew I couldn't let our moments end as such. I knew that there was more to it. At least I know you were able to listen and say the right words, even if they broke me. If nothing else…

A Man If West Destiny

To all of them not me,

Thinking of You

She shuts her eyes when you're inside
It's you that she won't see
She bites her lip and rides it down
Because she thinks of me
And all the ways we use to touch the smiles she
hides inside and such
These aren't the things you get from her 'cuz
I'm the guy that she'd prefer
One day she will realize I'm where she wants to
be
That's why she always runs away and then
comes back to me
Yeah, I know she's off with someone new
Because she doesn't feel much worth
She never got her daddy's love but there's more
that she deserves
She shuts her eyes when you're inside
It's you that she won't see
She bites her lip and rides it down
Because she thinks of me
She lies when she lies in bed and spreads her
legs for you
Because she thinks that you can do the things
that I can do
But she won't find her daddy's love at the end
of your bedpost
During all her needful times I'm who she thinks
of most
But I can't let go of my pride and she can't
stand me being right
And so, each night each nigh each night
I tell my Self that's why
She shuts her eyes when you're inside

A Man If West Destiny

It's you that she won't see
She bites her lip and rides it down
Because she thinks of me
She likes to have what she calls fun but its
deeper than you know
You think you're on the upper side, but the
South is where she goes
To return into these arms, a familiar song for us
to dance
But she still don't understand that she's had her
last chance
She shuts her eyes when you're inside
It's you that she won't see
She bites her lip and rides it down
Because she thinks of me
So, watch her eyes they're only lies when she
says that you're better
For she's already thought of me and all the ways
to bed her
So, she shuts her eyes
She shuts her eyes
She shuts her eyes
When you're inside

Thinking of You

No, seriously,

    to V,

        Who lives in a world where
        I do not exist.

        Enjoy.

A Man If West Destiny

Let me tell you what an oxbow is
The living earthly thing of what I represent
Molded from a river's ebb and flow
How it comes
How it goes
How it came
How it went
From many singled spiked moments
Where the water's anger builds to thrash
and pushes on the edge
and bends it to another path
More like a fork in the road
Much like which is not known
Now the river must decide
The raging flow or still water
Which side?
The river does flow to both
Because it can
Mother Nature need not understand
It has been and it is
Important in all it gives
It was once in land that is not seen
Not able to tell that it has been
It thrived in land that could be dead
Withered from not making bed
And not being nourish-ed
But always was and is
And will always cradle
The river up ahead

Thinking of You

Perfectly
You are
I'm here on my knees
Perfectly
Help me to stop
I'm here on my knees
Perfectly where I am
I'm here on my knees
Perfectly
Because I make you cry
I'm here on my knees
Perfectly
Ask me to stop
I'm here on my knees
Perfectly
The beat will drop
I'm here on my knees
Perfectly
Perfectly
Ask me to stop?
Ask me to stop
Where I am
I'm here on my knees
Perfectly
I will not stop
Forever on my knees

A Man If West Destiny

You got the rush
I give the thrust
You give the push [push away]
I get the crush
Crush of my heart under all my sin
I'm too good for the pressure
To break skin and take it all in
As you're pretty sure
We both could use nourishment
You would rather trek on your own
With your hungry eyes
Then I'll as I am; and fend alone
I'm just starving for your attention

Thinking of You

The fire of this Sagittarius
has not yet burned enough
but think this the water
to which she will be snuffed?
Certain patterns of the elements
have chains that act against their peers
The water within me gives
the spark for her fire to persevere
The thing needed to give an eclectic burn
The wind within me gives the fuel
for which her
flameful licks will yearn.
A rainbow of sight and heat not felt before
Beauty from unhindered chaos
Let the heavens pour
Let them pour for what's in store
To be each other's opposite
In their eyes they still adore
unhindered chaos
To set it afire, let it pour

You know who knocks upon your door
You know what I'm knocking for
Permit my entrance if you perceive
So, into the night us two will leave
Never knowing what's in store
Never caring and just wanting more
Onward to my chamber room
As each other's hold consumes
the substance you must flame to burn
Only your permittance heeds
the rolling waves to turn

A Man If West Destiny

I'm some immune
to poison on your lips
So how do you fair against the cold daggered steel of
the diction I twist?
Straight to the heart
My words do not miss
So, I must be wary when the butterfly
and the flower embrace in a kiss
Straight to the heart
Forever I am cursed to do this
But her...
A rogue by any other name
Would she kill as sweet?
Poisoned kiss upon the lips of steel
Pierced through my heart's defeat
A she you ask?
For only her can fulfill the task
complete like no other
Behead
post bed
Don't befriend this lover
There is no worry in the shadows
Though there really should be
This is where she likes to step
then act out maliciously
Not strong or not aware
Just more strain for her to care
Fall not deep in attempt to stare
For my fate you too will share
Deep she'll peer into your eyes
As she stabs you in the back
Because Death is not within her grasp
But worse off if your life should last

Thinking of You

It's called oxytocin
You release it when you're close to him
That's how with such ease
On your back and your knees
You return after time and again to be pleased
Creased in the folds
of each time you hold
you tell me to let go
but don't lie cuz we know
All the way through the bittersweet end
how you return to your childhood friend
I'm being now
Still much like a kid
So, I ask of you
when will we begin?
That's the wonderful thing
about this notion called change
It will take flight
When you don't want the same
But first that emotion needs to be sent
Then you will notice this difference
So yeah, I'm standing
In front of you
To be the that first step
For your breakthrough
And after all this happy occurs
Already you'll be towards your future
The first step in your little world
is taking that leap right over me little girl
And after that if you do jump back
Then you're back in the same
And that same is the past

A Man If West Destiny

So, let us begin in the swallows of my bed
To show what it is like to get head
from a head
Heart from a heart
Cock from a cock
Lie back my dear and just play your part
Boob from a boob
Poltroon from poltroon
Don't feel too used
For I'm coming soon
Not too early
No not like that
Though I'm still not conceited
I'm coming to give you just what you needed
Coming in time for the roles to reverse
Sitting high on the throne is your little skin purse
The place where I deposit
Or am able to exchange
Stick my head in and forever am changed
My time is my money
Invested with proper interest
Buying happiness, but now
back to business
More of these streets
in due time I will own
I'm wealthy beyond means
Care for a loan?

Thinking of You

I'm too much before
Ohhh yeah
She's too much after
Ohhh yeah
There's just before
skipped
right to the after
There is just us
without the laughter
Ohh yeah
Ohh yeah

Baby I could kiss like this every day
What makes you think that
just because you're gone
my talents gone away?
Seduction is a hobby
Passion's always been a forte
Because of the right Influences
The right Influenced living
leads Influenced styles
So, when you're
In-flu-enced
Give Influenced smiles

A Man If West Destiny

Crossing the line's
still crossing the line
Whether you're one inch
or one mile over
With me
Is with me
Whether You are afraid
Or you
let me do better
With you
Is with you
Whether I bed you now
Or you
show me later
Crossing the line's
still crossing the line

Read on this
to know how exactly I have felt
How just one little look
would make my heart's wall melt
So, you can no longer say
"'tis the drugs that make you sad
but 'tis the dreams that come and tell
the lifetimes the two of us have had."
Sad for they were only dreams

Thinking of You

No no
Surreal is an understatement
How the hell
We just came and went
I want that last caress
I need not to miss your skin
I gaze on thee with non-venomed eyes
Every catch like the first time again
So, I won't hear that you
won't hear me
I won't crave my breath down the sheets
As yours down my back
I won't put you on the pedestal
I won't do the things you're supposed to
I won't notice just how good you are
I won't believe in rules
I won't believe in or what you do
but I still won't tell them your truth
Because if nothing else
then I'll still say
"If nothing else…"
Then we'll still play
If nothing else
Give me a chance
before you give me a change

A Man If West Destiny

Your lips
Like the quiver
where my arrows live
With the unsteadiness that each one gives
Through the echoes my demands are sent
in restless stills within the wind
Perfected time I control and take
Each stroke a strike
Bullseye and mate
Checked from whence the words do make
Each stroke a strike
My gives will take
For I hit my mark
Because I aim to please
I shoot the straightest even down on my knees
Straight from the hip
with precision and care
A volley of stone soaring through errs
A maker with peace
then change is becoming
It doesn't seep pain
If you don't have it coming
This is the "hurt" that doesn't leave scars
No, it doesn't leave scabs
This is the "hurt"
Everyone wishes they had

Thinking of You

Poetry is queer
Every word and rhyme you hear
Poetry will always be queer
If we are the things that we truly eat
What then are the things of which we truly speak
upon the things which our ears will truly feast
Dine now and enjoy
Poetry is queer

Walk with me awhile
You know how I make you smile
Returning Favors
Like that which you aren't aware
I know the shadows up ahead
That is where I'm from my dear
So, no need to be scared
Black lit play is ever great
but not as great as sunlit ways
More muscles for the way you live
(A frown)
and less work to do with what I give
(A smile)
If you walk with me a while
Just walk with me a while
I know how you make me smile

A Man If West Destiny

Let go   let go
You think you know love?
Well then let it go
Don't get the burn as it yearns to
not let go the rope
If I love myself
If I love myself
How to let go too
Where first then was the rope,
fashioned as a noose?
If I love myself
If I love myself
It's me that I'm to hold
I'll no longer hold myself
But how then will I know
where to return if I let go the rope?
I'll admit I'm somewhat lost
in "looking" to know love
I'm sure not to hold too long
to lose myself in these ways
So, I let go of me
too much some would say
Let go   let go
The majority parade
If I love myself
I should really let go
But others in this case
just as great have simply all said no
If first the Sun had been refused
then who if any, if no Galileo, as well
I'll let go yes, I'll let go
of this beam and rope
and live a different hell

Thinking of You

Baby I know everything is fragile to you
Maybe to blame because I can see through you
I don't believe that you are made of glass
The light that refracts has potential to last
If you don't give out the hate you receive
I'll show you how
If you just believe
The sands of time have weathered you tough
Things always get better
My diamond
My diamond in the rough

I think of her
In lilies and lace
I think of her
Legs wrapping my face
I think of her
Arching her back
I think of her
Contorting her waist
I think of her
Springing the well
I think of her
To savor the taste
Until she pulls me out
Another two-sided embrace

A Man If West Destiny

I can't say hello again
    when there was no bye
I'm sorry I wasn't
    strong enough that nite
Going nowhere was best
for her
But not good enough to say
We are best at what we hate
But the time it takes to get that way
Could have been spent in better play
To better you
For some would say
Thus, I can't say bye

Loe Loe Loe
All that I can sing.
Loe Loe Loe
She whistles through the wind.
Loe Loe Loe
The way she moves.
Loe Loe Loe
All I hear without the V.

Thinking of You

Take me down to see the fields
I've not seen it before
Kill it red
Kill it red
Why would I
Why Would You
Kill us red
Kill us true

One day of rest
Turned into many
Weeks on end
Turn years into plenty
Still none the further
I'll always pursue her
Hungry as a pack
Pounce
Attack
And do more than chew her

A Man If West Destiny

Her waistline is a refuge
I wanna suff
Suff
Suffocate you
On my way inside to hate you
Down the rabbit hole
I chase you
Catch up and break you
Nothing left for him to rescue
She said
"No, no not a nerve
But you did touch something."
That's what she said
I wanna touch it all
From crust to meringue
And all outside
And all underneath

Tell me what it's like to be you
Wanting to be someone
Like me
Trying to be
Someone for you
So, know that when it rains
It is because of me
My heart is full of tears and pain
Because we cease to be

Thinking of You

Before these thoughts there have been no cure
More oft than not I've been too sure
That I
I am the butterfly
I am the butterfly
Who dreamt of being a man
As a butterfly I can enjoy
The many tastes of life's nectars
From all the gardens 'round the world
I'll have all of the flowers, so sweet
As a man I can enjoy
Living
One life
Loving
One love
Oh, we're complete
But as I am
I can only enjoy
Being stuck inside this web
All wrapped up my heart and head's cocoon
I hope to see you soon
Because I
I am the butterfly
I am the butterfly
Who dreamt of being a man
I can only dream to be a man
I can only dream to be a man
I can only dream to love just one
I can only dream to be a man

A Man If West Destiny

Keep her to the end?
I'll keep my flask and pipes as friends
They may run out (as well) sometimes
They never let me down
But when she runs out at night
She's all over town

Great to see you
How have you been?
Can't help myself that it's great to be seen
I'm keen on you
But you're unseen
Lost inside the glamour and always on scene
I may be a kandy kid
Hell, you, kid your scene
Is being seen
and always on scene

Even though you may be scared
It only means you're not prepared
It never says that it's not there
when you hold my hand
You have two hearts that I have seen
An unfinished book I opened (you) that
I'd like to read
And savor on these lips as well
As I read, you tell yourself
the sound that falls upon these ears
as I chime your little bell
When you hold my hand

Thinking of You

I'll lie to you as you to me
Tell me that you care to hear
So that my words flow free
Hold the truth that could be you;
the Topic of each Phrase.
I said and say them to be golden
Now wonder if all the ticks throughout all time
were your thoughts they were holding
These all have been my past
Loving thoughts of you is a future you must too
to show the gold inside from the things you do

Actions make up what we do
Goes on inside the bedroom too
This with me is how
I've come about defining you
because your actions there are
proving that the apple's fall
was close
but the roll was a bit more than far
I now see
why you often say
you're just a falling star
burned out and burning
burned out not burning on
And such
And such
So, on and on

A Man If West Destiny

She wants the boa
Like a feather
Pin her down with ease of touch
A gentle hold to keep her there
And such
And such
And so on and forth
Oxymoronic?
More off or more on it?
I can't tell, I just can't tell
If we're gonna play in the bedroom
Opossum's a game you can play by yourself

My little girl
When will you learn?
Yes, another lesson
(yes, something that you don't deserve)
Maybe I didn't deserve you then
But you still deserve to be happy
And now we don't deserve to be friends
Happy none of us will be
if we refuse
to learn the gifts given
to help us prove
that what we go through
is more than less the use

Thinking of You

I don't ever have that much to say
But will you save one dance today
One dance with me
And nothing more
Remember how we do
When it's just me and you
One dance saved for just us two
This night and this floor
I won't let him see
How you truly are with me
How I'll always make you cry
Because we never said goodbye
For all the reasons that you kick yourself
for booting me for things that I can't help;
WHEN I AM AROUND YOU
So please keep holding on to that memory
Of how you and I do
For it is the simplest things in life that's free
The simplest things that are the greatest
When you add them all up
Why, these are the things that make us

A Man If West Destiny

All I hear is save me
Save me
Save me
But I'm barking up the wrong tree
Got the wrong castle in front of me
Fight the fight
Make the flight up I do
Just to find that you
aren't the right princess
Aren't the right princess for me?
But I won this fight
I don't waste my time
I made the flight
To a castle
A castle in the sky
I'm so very high
and standing at the gates
weaponic words in tow
never sure of the challenges I face
but I'm always ready for a test
Somehow, I find the castle
but never the right princess
onward
forward
upward
backward
stab and slash
the dragons down
behind the gate they're slain
Slaughtered for the next man
Because he has a "better" plan
for a princess not for me

Thinking of You

She   noticed me walking
She hasn't noticed   on by without her
Walking on by   and all her troubles
Without her   troublin' for some
Troubles troublin'   for some time
For some time   sometime to myself
For some time   alone and a lone
My self alone   searching for her
A lone searching   and all her troubles
For her

Along you merried down your path
When come across you did of me
Now alone you merry off
And thus aroused my jealousy
For soon you'll come to find
A truer, loving heart in another man
Than you found in mine
Time will pass, eventually
And maybe I'll be well
But as you left with onward steps
I traced them and I fell

A Man If West Destiny

Number one stud
No, number one loser
Stuck in first place
Because I can see through her
My eyes stare back at me
She don't know what she want
She just wants to have fun
She should know all I want
She should just let me come
And go
Come and go
Come   and   Go

She stated under
all those stars
"You're the brightest one so far.
But I know there's better."
Not Mr. No
More like Mr. Right not now

I only dream in colors
I can read inside them too
All the signs and no words
They pointing me to you
Wanna see your wavelengths tied in knots

Thinking of You

First then, then, then this
She walked away
….no last bye
….no last kiss
"I don't blame you."
That's all she said
I'll test out
        And push you away
She want me back
She want me back
Not all the way
Just half
Just half
Half of that
That you was
She walked away
Just because

Did I, did I
Did I ever say?
Harmful things that'll make you go away
Did I, did I
Did I ever hear you say
Pleasant songs that would make me stay?
Bruises
because you like the pain
Fire on roses
Melting hearts that stray

A Man If West Destiny

She is a hands-on art museum
I can't look
and not touch
I can't be a friend as such
Before me she just kept changing
After me she just wants
The same thing
The thing that she should see
The boy she wants
must be better than me
She couldn't figure out this figure
So fast in time
She just went bye

I'm sorry what they did to you
You really think that I'd
     be better too?
But why must I apologize
'twas you that fell for all their lies
Enough baggage on your back
I won't pick up those poser's slack
Why would I want any of that
You simply planned to be
out of my league

Simpatico exist chance
Is really use us less (useless) trance
If there's no resistance
Then there's no existence

Thinking of You

Snapshot of our lips on mine
Stitch in time
You saved me nine
Worth more than a thousand
Time in stitches
Backed to you
Worth more than a thousand
I'm only halfway through
Only one way to do it
I'll show you how
No time to be scared
The time is now
Look all around
This is the middle
But it'll not be real far
A little corny but not cliché
If you show me yours
I will show you my ways

When will we get there?
Well, where the hell are we to be?
I'll find out when you do
All of this is news to me
I'm sleeping light years in head
Your body's just around the bend
Both our hearts in tomorrow
Awaiting notes that we're to send
So when will we get there?
When do you plan to leave
You got some major tracking
If you wanna catch up to me

A Man If West Destiny

All this for a girl
I'd set fire to the world
Yours precious yours
Mine; can't burn what's been scorched
So yeah, lil' darling
All this for a girl
Perfectly the beat did drop
And you could hear a pin fall
All the little boys come running
at their mommy's call
Lights are low and shadows high
Now the time for creeps
Now the time for me
Now the time to lease
Now the time to be
All the evils, all the spooks
They rush to me
I'll spread the word
All the land burning
I set fire to it
Yes sir, cuz a girl
No flame will live where it has already burned

Thinking of You

Still don't know how to be a man
All I knows to make a stand
Just put your back against the past and go-o-o
Don't let it take you like it took me
Don't let it shake you like it shook me
Girl, I know you're feeling lonely
But sadly, you're not the only
Just put your back against the past and go-o-o
Don't let it take you like it took me
Don't let it shake you like it shook me
You pout and shout
That it's not fair
From what life my dear
Do you compare
And make such a contrasting view
My only strength can come from you
If you just
If you just
Just put your back against the past and go-o-o
Don't let it take you like it took me
Don't let it shake you like it shook me
The last thing that you'd like to do
Is hear words that are so cruel
But once you push
And once you go
All the tears that you let flow
Are dying in this tragedy you know
Just put your back against the past and go-o-o
Just put your back against the past and go-o-o

A Man If West Destiny

Here she comes
Time slows down to a unified beat
No, she flies away
I leap towards the average pace
Now another
The world disappears in a blur
Closer, closer we become
Until her eyes rest above
Her wings send her past
I stupor back from drunkenness
I've got to get her
'Cuz everyone's a junkie
Can't lose this one
'Cuz everyone's a junkie
I grab hold and bring her down
Alone we pulse and dance we alone
Lost in touch
Down I weigh anxiety
Her got to go
Junkie is everyone
Up give up
Junkie is everyone

Thinking of You

One day I think I could wise up
But now I'm tuned
To us tied up
On your lips again
On your lips again I wish
The fall too fast
The star did crash
On your lips again
I'm sure we'd last
Always new
Every time
Grow to grew
With You in mind
I know it hurts
To pull the scabs
A tougher heart
Is what you have
All with You in mind

Thank God I never met you
Before tonite otherwise I
I'd be better off not knowing
All the ways you say goodbye
But my little smiles begin to
Crack on through this vertigo
Counterclockwise spins truly
Get you off but now it's time to go
I want to love you
I want to love you cuz you're bad
You say you want it deeper
I give it hard
It's much too fast

A Man If West Destiny

Don't take the fall
For not keeping the leash
Unwrap the binds
Unleash the BEAST
Soon you will find
The nature of that
Discomfort in hope
As honey from wax
One bee
One queen
One bee
Sometimes more at a time
Loyal?
Don't care
Sometimes more at a time

Round eyed girl with
A song in her name
Works behind the coffee stand
She said,
"Oh no oh no my man.
Why are you so lonely?"
I said,
"Don't you, don't
You don't see
That pretty little girl standing next to me
Because I can't see that she's left me
So please don't call me lonely"

Thinking of You

Your little box
Pandora
I fished around and hunted down
The essence of your core
All the things that did escape
Well, Lesser men
Would seem to hate
Then, crawled out the box
Some hope to walk the land
Sadly, she encountered
The box of a devilish man
And opened up his box
Amongst the glam our little hope got lost

Come hold my hand
I'm gonna take you away
Away from what you've known
If this is out there
Imagine what the world has told
To many others like ourselves
But never ventured a tale to tell

A Man If West Destiny

Oh, the chase
But it must be done
The game is afoot
I am a head
You're just a heart
That I can move
But you're too weighed down
Drained and bled
Bled out and purged
A fallen you
Has now emerged
Through your own ashes
Again, your fire will burn

I am the skip before the stone
I make the ripples
But all you see there
is the thing that you've thrown
I did this and do
Because I'm running from you
You catch up
In another form
Can't make out how
I become the stone and drown

She'll do anything (I'll say anything)
Just gotta make the first move
She'll do anything (I'll say anything)
She's always in the mood
She'll do anything (I'll say anything)
We're lying when we're lying

Thinking of You

All of me
Just what you see
In front of thee
Just wait and see
I'm Mr. Saturday Lover
When weeks end is over
A daily friend
'tis nothing for her
Wait and see her Saturday Lover

You can run away from this
Be scared, have fear
When you hear
That it's love
But know it's from me
And can only be one way
And that is it's tough
Not sure what it takes to be him
I'm here for just one reason
If you can't see it
I'm not sure you ever will
None of that matters
Because I'll love you still

Yes, you can I know
One day the most beautiful bride
You know that you're ready
When you're happy inside
For you to be happy
It may take a while
But the first step on that path
Is to have a genuine smile

A Man If West Destiny

Everything costs too much
Too much exertion on my insides
Wanting to break free
To take you somewhere else
Transported physically
That is how this curse feels
I want to so much
My soul is taxed involuntarily
I see in your eyes what we could have been

I've flown some
Fallen
Spread my wings and flew
Somehow on this perch
I'm resting next to you
You need to fly
You've got to learn
But it doesn't have to be goodbyes
See I've made concern
with the heavens, but first the sky
Spread your wings it's time to learn
We'll rise through the ashes
but first we've got to burn
Midnite oil
Pressed against me
Midnite oil
Released from you to me
In your arms
Once again

Thinking of You

Tell me how we could
How we could be friends
In your arms once again
Perfect practice is perfect
but I need repetition
My pillow would like to plea its case
If you would just listen
When I said are you in (R-U-N)
She said OK then
I'll be leavin'
I scare you
Well, I scare me
How do you think I feel?
Tempested feelings while soul gentile
I'll not tread where presence unwelcome
Three years I've fought
But still must I chase the sun
More like chasing, chasing this want
Chasing this need
I'll never achieve

No good deed goes unpunished
as the bad ones benefit too much
The magic pricked from one of your thorns
Is heavily worth the touch
While ignoring selfless pain
is forcing crimsoned rush
I must inspect and utilize my time
To see your clocking's tick
Time is but an essence and
Stalls to feel the clicks

A Man If West Destiny

Be careful in trusting
what you hear, what you see
Be careful in wanting fairy tales
or wishing make believe
Some may not envision the same dreams
Or have the will like yours
All they'll do is fake it
Magic creates a joyful life
All depends on how you make it
Magic can be dark
and will manifest its greed
like its happy counterpart
One thought is a seed
Nor does it need much nourishment
Even beauty comes from weed
And yours should be kept
But doesn't have to be sealed in a jar
Forever will your beauty be
Like the twinkling of the stars
The falling ones have beauty too
But watch then what you wish at least
I'll adore you from afar
As you've wished me the BEAST

Thinking of You

Because if nothing's new
then nothing's changed
Which means your unhappiness is still the same
May these words now be a spark
A catalyst within your heart
Wherein resides the flame of hope
to show you through the dark
Having fear is ok my dear
So long as it does not lurk and leer
and linger on to take control
beating down on you its hold
Something you don't want, I know
What I do of what you need
is freedom for your fire to breathe
The substance that you need to burn
is something you yourself must earn
to keep eternal fire and not scorch this world
You can't burn what already has been set aflame(me)
So, you must reignite yourself again, again to walk
in smothered warmth that roars and lets you live
So, I leave and leave these words
Do well with this spark I give
You do not need to be saved
But to shine your light you must be brave

A Man If West Destiny

Through the sun's night fall
we'd dance
As we did then in the rain
As we did in joyful song and did in painful glance
Not a friendship there was gained
How none before had yet explained
You can't be friends
No not when all you feel
Not when all you sang
No, you can't be friends
When all is joy and pain

Perfectly
Because
You can walk away from me
I'm here on my knees

Where The 101 Continues…

To my siblings J.D. & Jessika, who believed in a path for me

To Ventura County, California, who gave me a path

To all those 'her,' for giving me a reason to stay the path

1 - A Gift's Responsibility
by Gerome Mauricio

The young boy tried to avoid Show & Tell for as long as possible. His mother poor, father absent. Nothing he had to bring from home was special enough. He didn't have fancy electronics, advanced gaming systems, a trip to tell of, or a pet to bring.

The other children giggled as he stood up for his turn. He nervously approached the front of class and wrote his last name on the chalkboard. The boy explained that that is all he's been given in this world. With pride swallowed he said, "It's my duty to create a legacy, not uphold one."

2 - Creative Righting Technique
by Aaron Knout

The principal paused outside the classroom to hear the speech being given by the student. "...the social system's structures have inequities inherently embedded..."

The principal interrupted, asking that their English teacher be excused to converse outside the classroom. The door shut behind them.

"This will get us in some serious trouble once parents hear what is being taught in your class." the principal spoke with a small glare.

"I'm not teaching anything out of the ordinary. This is simply a writing exercise. The students are reading what they wrote. Are you afraid people will be upset over *fiction*?" He emphasized sarcastically.

3 - Greetings Carte Blanche
by Gerome Mauricio

He wasn't alone "living" inside the closet. He obsessed of coming out, nothing else. He was cornered by his own indecisiveness. Others could live freely through his sacrifice. Nay they WOULD!

The voices suggested he come out already. Been too long. *Enough*! Silence was needed now. Refusing this hidden lifestyle, courage coursed throughout. He opened up, sweat dripping profusely, throat cleared, announcing himself. All heads were simultaneously attentive. Never was he so popular. Words were obviously meaningless. They immediately knew.

He relaxed. Long-lasting serenity! Hopefully, those behind him running past desired their life more than the zombies unappeasably tearing into him.

4 - Please, Nothing Personal
by Miss Ahjanee

In a fabled area of the forest overlooking a lake, a scorpion and frog unfortunately witness a natural occurrence.

He twitched on an altar, her web. Each action worsened his situation. She remained safe; tactically encroaching. He pleaded. Yes, some suffered from his spinning. These were desperate times. He beggingly wriggled for freedom, vowing to not be so careless. She vowed to not let this one get away. Her hypnotizing eyes paralyzed him. Nothing could be done. Teasingly, she asks him, "Any last words?"

He looked around, no objection for rescue. He stared back at her, finally giving in. "I do."

5 - Dear Georgia [O'Keeffe] Obsession Some
by Miss Ahjanee

He travelled over mountain sides, deserts, swamplands, and curvy coastlines but nothing compared to being Downtown. There all the lilies hung upside down. He made sure to stop and smell these flowers. Spread wide they persevered the bustle to come out to the desire within the night.

    Some were seen heights away from the sewer's echo. Some window displayed for show. Others tried growing in alleys. He never understood the lilies sold on the street when beautiful petals still rose through its cracks. Each Downtown lily was ambitiously and individually bound. Regardless, he always leaned in forwardly to caress a blush.

Where The 101 Continues…

6 - A Patriot's Hill
by Aaron Knout

Jack and Jill stormed Capitol Hill to bring their king to lead

For they related all too well in hateful speech and greed.

But Jack and Jill marched on that Hill way past the eleventh hour.

The feeble tries of 'passersby' couldn't return their king to power.

So, Jack and Jill spoke on a hill saying the king's to blame.

The king just cried, telling lies, and denied all of his shame.

With Jack and Jill jailed on a hill, for years the country knew but could not see

There is no need for a goddamn king in a fucking democracy.

7 - I'm Migrant
by Aaron Knout

{English Translation}

Whomever finds my body, have the mercy to notify my phone's emergency contacts.

I've traversed the tribulations of terrains. I've endured the sun, days without food or water, and hidden from local gangs and deceptive smugglers; all for the destination's riches.

Everyone knows immigrants were America's foundation, but what more needs to be built? I promised a better future. One away from surging populations, increasing crime rates, and resource shortages.

I've crossed the border and am headed to a land unknown to me. I miss my family in California. I'll make a new home for them outside the U.S.

Where The 101 Continues…

8 - The Tortas and the Hair
by Gerome Mauricio

The hare shaded himself beside the food truck alongside the race's course. He leered, spotting the tortoise delayed in the distance.

While checking on his social media updates, he beamed. "Already 1,000 furvorites for my starting line selfie!"

Many savory bites relished into his merited meal, he twitched at a strand in his food. "Is this fox?!" He fumed at the cook that his abased review would have lasting effects.

"Sir, your shoulder. Hug any fans?" The cook pointed.

"Yeah, well uh…" Clarity roused, the hare glanced behind for the tortoise, but only found him advanced and crossing the finish line.

9 - Just Ice
by Gerome Mauricio

"People fished here?" the boy asked.

"Many things have changed." Answering his captivated grandson; both pondering the pier's decades long renovations to accommodate rising sea levels.

"What happened?"

"That's complicated." He reminisced.

"Like bullying? [Shifting anxiously] Didn't you help?"

The elder exhaled patient digression while clarifying glaciers, extinction, and what chocolate was; sharing homemade cricket flour cookies. "Imagine Nature's cookie jar. We argued instead of saving enough of the cookies we wanted. So now there's only raisin cookies."

"Ewww. Sour grapes!"

"They aren't all sour. [Pointing] San Francis 'Island' formed beautifully despite endeavors diverging the refuse." Pacific waves echoed turbulent tranquility.

Where The 101 Continues…

10 - LBD
by Miss Ahjanee

He found her in the walk-in closet, still deciding what to wear.

"What do you think?" she asked, "This one or this one?" She held up two similar black dresses.

"Don't say they look alike" He thought. "The one on your left." he responded.

She chose the one on her right. "Ugh. Men don't worry about such things." She slighted.

"Not so true. A man's word is his LBD; styled perfectly to fit any occasion and sometimes the only resort. Oh, btw, as 'promised' I'm dressed and ready before you finished."

Now he waits for her hair, makeup, then shoe matching.

11 - Hands Around the World United
by Gerome Mauricio

"No, It's fine. I'll sleep when I'm dead. Let's continue. You never know. One easily affects another. Besides, the flight won't be that long."

"Traveling overseas isn't...? Never mind. What did you like best about Research?"

"Working with hazardous materials. I mean, exposing certain chemicals to oxygen will violently set them on fire. Even the smallest amount!"

"Really?!!"

"Education is a rabbit hole."

"Why did you leave?"

"Honestly? Politics. Blah Blah. My personal beliefs led me to my calling."

"Which is?"

"Chemicals. But different. Here, *sample* lotions still work. Underwear Bombers ruin it! Lollygaggers!"

"Sealed. May I?"

"Thought you'd never ask."

12 - First Impressions
by Miss Ahjanee

She was beautiful. He struggled with eye contact as she initiated conversation. Whatever. His applied efforts resulted no interruptions. Her numerous "first times" prior were no concern. His confidence masking nervousness. He needed what she needed to give. Simple enough, but minimum standards aren't considered.

    Could he possibly fill her void? Every response she smiled; listening closer, eyes widening, anxiously giving subtle hints only to retreat. 'Cat and mouse' between the two. This challenged both their inhibitions. However appealing, she could control any situation. She thanked his efforts. He stood slowly afterward, silently questioning her words, leaving the office. "Other applicants?"

13 - Finders Keepers
by Gerome Mauricio

"The medical achievements can rid all of the cancer." the teen begged his grandfather.

He replied, "I know I can opt out. I wish you could understand. Several family members died from diverse types when I was young. Back then people suffered more than what I'm now willing. I'm not sure if I found cancer or if cancer found me. I want to share with you the anticipation of loss."

"Why couldn't you just impart wisdom and live longer?"

"Wisdom? Of the three kinds of people in this world: some are never meant to keep, some are meant to never find."

14 - 'dence Audition
by Miss Ahjanee

Many parenting techniques allow approaches accumulating into two different 'dence forms. Natural that one 'parent' is better at one practice than the other.

    Some 'parents' excel in teaching both 'dence styles, some pay others to teach their offspring, some do both without a partner, and some will teach nothing.

    He had to be an unconventional tenderfoot; having only his mother to learn from. She lacked proper directive herself.

    The man now had to perform for the world, expressing proficiency. Prowess in one manifests adeptness in the other. Both give poise to take lead. Time for his presentation of Confidence and Independence.

15 - Governing Omnipotent Deity
by Gerome Mauricio

An Atheist, Agnostic, and Believer were summoned to a place outside their perception. Their astonishment transformed fear into composure.

Around them were the omniscient gods from all the religions. A representative approached the three, informing them they were there to choose the next in control.

Each attempted to speak out. The only words achieved were of that in unison from all three. "How are we to decide?" Their question echoed, silencing the floor.

Knowing how to proceed, they searched within themselves. Through much deliberation, the god ultimately agreed upon by the three resembled a mirror.

The other deities sighed in relief.

Where The 101 Continues…

16 - Passage
by Gerome Mauricio

Mr. Costman answered the door, and then dropped to his knees at gunpoint. Assembly Guards. Elite.

"Leah Lynn is declared 'Fit for Society.'" one said.

Her Hormonal Disposition Report was shown. Authentic government seal. Her mother begged repeatedly, "NO! TOO YOUNG!"

"No warning? What did Mom know?" Leah thought.

Leah was taken; handcuffed, gagged, and blindfolded. She was unbound at their 'Maturation Center,' then escorted down hallways. She saw numbered doors. 213.

Leah was pushed in. Soft music. Candles. Some unknown boy. He sat tense, nervous, on a lavishly styled bed. The door locked from outside, confining them together. Leah trembled.

17 - No, Child Left Behind
by Miss Ahjanee

Whom better to protect the borders than those born and raised within. A sense of pride was carried by all working the walls, also heavy artillery and more than enough ammunition.

Three borders of walls and the Gulf made the fourth. Sometimes walls work both ways. Desperation shared amongst those foolish and those brave.

A few men from a well-trained militia was all it took to catch movement on the Western wall, even through pouring rain.

"Well, another young one." A soldier trying to make sense of everything.

"I can't have another baby." the frightened girl pleaded, "Please let me leave."

18 - Against the Wind
by Gerome Mauricio

It's not so much a matter of right and left. For one's right is left to another. But what is left to one isn't necessarily another man's right. Thus, he set forth to see what is left after finding what is right to him.

Sometimes he found himself on what he thought was the right side. Reality quickly showed him which side. Forcing him to rise up again. He pushed, fighting arduously to not trip from obstacles and hazards before him.

Try as he might, whenever the wind blew he would fall, always landing on the wrong side of the fence.

19 - Lips Serve Us
by Miss Ahjanee

His first look is for a ring. The next are her eyes. His focus was drawn to her speech. Her mouth contorted, vibrating rapid waves exiting her mouth. The noises around them drowned out.

Barely attending to what she was saying, he could only hone in on her enlarged lips. She noticed his gaze. She touched her hair, playfully. Their pause added levity. She continued listing options for his enjoyment.

Back to watching her. He wondered the lipstick's name. How would it taste? He glanced again into her eyes, peering deeper.

"Sir? Sir? Those are the Specials. Dining in or takeout?"

20 - A Tree Plainly
by Gerome Mauricio

It was the last Great Tree of the last Great Forest of the North. Now it was his turn. He'd waited for his meeting with the dying tree.

He approached with his arms widened for embrace as tears fell. "You're supposed to outlive us. We need you. What are we to do? How could you just decide to go?"

The tree looked down. "So many questions. Your time's about up. We're leaving for a higher cause."

"But why?"

"Because."

"You can't give up!"

The tree's laugh bellowed, rustling it's leaves. "And what did the oceans have to say to such rhetoric?"

21 - Add Diction
by Aaron Knout

Accumulated paraphernalia complements his table. His lighter, a variable appendage with conditional surplus value, sparked the bong. The gist of smoke inhaled. Each lung expenditure increased his apartment's haze, positively amplifying mood. However culpable for minimal function, ongoing operations formulated his daily summation.

Pills plus powders were associated to gain "balance." "Supplements for whole results," He postulated. "otherwise I'm odd." He rationalized answers, not solutions.

Unbounded lips ascended the primed pipe flame combination. 'One more time.' Again. Twisting. (Cardinal property for integral distribution.) Compounded sequence extensions negated diminishing returns. His meaning, now, more than average: eked acts grossly progressing complex collectiveness.

22 - Strangers in the Night
by Miss Ahjanee

They were no longer unacquainted in the day. Coffee runs turned into walks, walks into dates, dates into romance; romance into an especially encumbering evening.

In bed, his left hand gently holding her neck. Curling their bodies, his right hand brushed her spine to lower back, marching his fingers, rounding her hips. Her arms enfolded, hands behind him. One loses sight of the other when getting close.

{Wet stab} Her words were a dagger in his back, turning deeper with each twist of diction. A rogue by any other name could not kill as sweet. Strangers remained strangers in the night.

23 - Body Shamed
by Miss Ahjanee

Specific traits were her measurement criteria for mate compatibility. Enough information can be gathered from observation.

The first date tests one's senses. How are things perceived? How is maintenance of the primary sensory organs: eyes, ears, mouth, and nose?

She inferred a good head sits on strong shoulders. Does he carry life's challenges and himself with proper posture? Next date, knees followed and brought forth the willingness to bend. Toes showed grooming and his power to remain balanced.

By the end of the third date, she is ready to find how *intimate* one is with their head, shoulders, knees, and toes.

Where The 101 Continues…

24 - A Simple Man's Redemption
by Miss Ahjanee

King Midas' claimed gift from Bacchus was contact containing value. The callous king's greed colored his cold heart with cruel causal conviction.

From castle corner to corner, he scurried about celebrating without caution as cushion to curtain turned gold. His covetous quickly cut to his core, completely connecting scheme to conniption cost. The 24 carat caress caged the sustenance craving king.

The king cried foul. Bacchus took back the wish less one consequence. The king's instructed curse cleansing river plunge reversed his touch.

The king's decree that value exists in all things carried through the kingdom. The repercussion? Aureate covered mistresses.

25 - Saved By The Bell
by Aaron Knout

The playground was full with the big kids. The oldest kid had a bigger little brother (different moms); he kept all the kids in check. Most of them.

The local bully would mess with a kid who was his neighbor. Often the older brother messed with his neighbors. Like the bully would.

One day things got bad for everybody. Everyone chose sides because of no apparent teachers overlooking. Dirt and several punches thrown. Things were about to get worse. Then the bell to return to class sounded.

["Grandpa, you mean that's when the aliens came?"

"Yes, granddaughter, then they saved us."]

26 - Two Heads Better Than One
by Gerome Mauricio

The grandfather told his grandson the story that was told to him and passed down for generations. He told of the fighting between two wolves within each of us; a light and dark wolf. He furthered the attributes given both and tasked him with feeding the light one in each moment.

Days later the grandson, feeling conflicted, returned. The grandfather questioned the spirit of a wolf not fed.

"But grandfather," the boy retorted, "both showed me strengths the other lacks. They share my heart between them and have the best intentions for me. The starve of one would surely starve me."

27 - K-no-w Love Lost
by Miss Ahjanee

"Hurts." she fussed.

"Good. We're doing it right." Will's grunts mimicked thrusting.

"No..."

"My No triumphs." Overpowering her, he muffled any resistance. Serendipitous lifelessness reflected clarity between their dilated pupils. Will stopped.

"Cut!" Director demanded answers.

"Isn't this exploitative?" Will panted.

"***This,*** is the Fourth Wall broken to shoot the damn scene. Because you're feeling sensitive?"

"I'll break a Fifth Wall if..."

"Not One More!" Director's Wilde interjection prioritized stillness about. "Decide to cease the moment or seize the day, but mold imitation elsewhere. We're paying bills."

Will contemplated the set, crew, cameras, then followers; eventually yielding to her guiding hand.

Where The 101 Continues…

28 - Three GOATs Gruff
by Gerome Mauricio

Shel Silverstein, Hunter S. Thompson, and William Shakespeare went looking for 'sweetgrass.' They made their way to the hillside. As they neared, a troll came from under the bridge.

"Enter net!" the troll roared, pointing to his net. The GOATs collected themselves.

"I'll leave a bad taste, surely the next will satisfy." said Shel. The troll let him pass.

"Saturated with life, I'd be toxic." said Hunter, allowed to pass.

"Enter net!" The troll rumbled louder; making declarations.

"What the fuck is the Internet?" said William.

Unbalanced, the troll fell, sinking forever into the digital stream. The GOATs smoked 'sweetgrass' peacefully.

29 - Dinner Date
by Miss Ahjanee

He adjusted his tie, nervously trying in the mirror. He wiped sweat from his brow and left the bathroom. He sat back down in the restaurant lobby, looking for 'her.'

He checked his phone for any messages. Nothing. She was currently fifteen minutes late. He noticed a new hostess, so he approached the station to inquire about while he was away.

"Excuse me. Hi. I was wondering if anyone else had checked in for the table?"

"Yes sir, of course, what is the name?"

"Leigh. Frank."

"No, not yet sir."

"You're sure? She said she had reservations.[rereading the text] …Oh."

30 - One Nightstand
by Miss Ahjanee

Her fingers blindly found the snooze button. Her eyes slowly focused on the time. Her smile stretched past her arms. How better to awaken than [with] memories of the night prior? Her nervous hands felt for the previous evening's lover. Not even a note.

Morning stretching finished, she begrudgingly made her bed. Then, a soft thud was heard. She picked up and fully examined the unfamiliar timepiece from the floor. "Definitely something worth coming back for." she murmured, walking to *her* side of the bed.

The drawer opened with fervor; <u>this</u> watch added to the eclectic sea of costly male accoutrements.

31 - A Special Moment's Remissness
by Miss Ahjanee

A specific message transmitted. A simple task asked respectfully in response. Sympathy's signaled assumption acknowledged supposed partnered partaking of pain.

Sometimes a weathered feather proves no better than ropes and leather when signing off on kink to ink for someone's pleasure.

Hot breaths fluttered down her nape from his roughness. She struggled to utter the smallest of submissions. Sweat slowly trickled across her succulent skin from gripping her soft shoulders. Simpatico succumbed to gasps mouthed in succinct synchronous silence. Syncopated suffocation successfully connecting will to these thrill seekers.

She released a tempered whimper from his licentious whispers, "Good girl. Keep resisting."

32 - Not Even Close
by Miss Ahjanee

"Would it hurt to clean up around the apartment?" she asked her boyfriend.

"I'm not as good as you are at that stuff."

"Every little bit helps."

"I'll keep to things I'm good at like barbeque, fixing things, and that kinda stuff."

"Oh, so I cook and clean because I'm better? Is that why you drive everywhere?"

"Yes. You get it." He smirked. "Same with power and politics. Few can get past equality and wield such hardships. It's waiting for you. Take it. When you're better at it."

"You know what else is gonna wait, until *you* get better at it?"

33 - Three Little Words
by Miss Ahjanee

"You're the brightest…," She looked up at him. "…one so far."

His face lit up more than she'd ever seen. But her delicately chosen statement reverberated through his bones. He stepped back from their embrace, dropping his arms beside him.

Her dark brown eyes a fathomable conveyance peering past his pupils, past ambition, to the depths of his soul's comprehension.

Love can be so powerful that it brings one to their knees. And three little words can be so powerful as to keep one there.

"Let me go." She looked down on him, pointed to her heart, turned around, parted company.

34 - REFUSE
by Gerome Mauricio

The smell on the streets was too overpowering. The disparaged and homeless littered along lanes and alleyways. Daytime activity was the only method because of the curfew.

Conspiracy theories arose from tent cities gone missing, lower class neighborhoods cleared out, and buildings demolished for new development. Out of sight, out of mind. The streets were clean and amazed the senses with purity.

It was an otherwise tranquil day at sea. Container ships from Asia continued nearing California's coastline. The multitudes of thousands discarded suffered as cargo on those ships. An involuntary approach to seeking asylum. Perhaps, an early act of war.

35 - The Mad Had-Her
by Miss Ahjanee

Teatime. Always time for tea. It was and always was time for tea. Also, the exact time she came and left.

Time to set. Time to reset. Time for tea. She was his. He had her. Such enjoyment. Such fulfillment. So much damn tea. Sugar lump. Reset. Tea. Sugar lump. Reset. The time flew and somehow was the same moment. All of the time. He had her. She was his. Teatime. Time to go.

Time was angry with him and only excited his madness. Same words. Same way. All the same. Back to having her. Back to losing her. More tea.

Where The 101 Continues…

36 - The Mythical "O"
by Miss Ahjanee

She had field experience, but only discovered traces of the treasure. He met her in the wild and they quickly began co-exploration.

She'd been ineffectively deep within the cave several times before. Her fancy new gadgets kept them near the entrance. Applying their findings, they climbed. There it was in front of them, an "Orgasm."

"There must be more around here." She ecstatically yearned. "We work well together, let's keep the lookout for more."

"I'm not so sure. I understood that we were hunting for the same thing. I'll continue searching elsewhere. I know a more "Organic" relationship can be found."

37 - Downtown Abby
by Miss Ahjanee

She had a doll face. Untroubled, almost pristine. Smile lines that told beauty's superficial stories of mastery. Her blue eyes were somewhere to lose oneself. Her hair long and golden. She wore it down and only put it up when handling business.

    She was agile, benefitting from healthy living inside and out. Her profession kept her mindful and gave perks for on the job accomplishments.

    She swallowed sperm for happiness or got creamed for glowing skin, never complaining about work. False claims maybe, but why ruin good things? She took it as a commission. Ready she turned on the red light.

Where The 101 Continues…

38 - The Gem in Eyes
by Gerome Mauricio

She never thought her twins would be adventurous as they were opposite. As they grew, her expectations mimicked those the world held standard.

The "older" continued this path, leading him overseas. He traversed the deserts fighting windmills. He returned with the glow of glory, fulfilling mother's hopes.

The other's search was more internal though his head was in the clouds. He spent many nights battling the status quo; gaining the spoils of such wars. Years passed before he left Lucy's Diamond Kingdom in the sky. The mother cried at his return, seeing the sparkle of love and life in his eyes.

39 - Since Ability
by Miss Ahjanee

    Since she was gone, he was unable to figure out when things turned.
    Since he had no timing, he was unable to figure out why it happened.
    Since he had no reasoning, he was unable to figure out where to go.
    Since he had no direction, he was unable to figure out what to do.
    Since he had no idea, he was unable to figure out how to move forward.
    Since he had no mindfulness, he was unable to figure out who he was.
    Since he had no identity, he was unable to figure out if he did really truly exist.

40 - Over That Hill
by Gerome Mauricio

His goal was to finally conquer that summit. It had always seemed distantly far. "One day. Not today." He would think.

Over the years other landmarks proved to be difficult or treacherous. Some journeys were accompanied by colleagues and peers. Other hills were similar to this one, solo.

Following goodbyes, he set forth for victory. Most make it over but remain so remote. Correlative contact is unknown to those still on this side. One way forward. No return trips.

He did it! Looking down the ridge he saw a slippery slope and ended up hitting every rock on the way down.

41 - Betwixt
by Gerome Mauricio

He climbed the dangerous paths up the steep mountain. He finally reached the old sage sitting upon a boulder, meditating.

"Come, I've been expecting one. What exactly do you seek?"

Catching his breath, the inquisitor approached. "Please, I want to know life's meaning. Maybe then I'll find mine."

"Ahh. Everyone asks the same question. Life is like throwing a rock into fog."

"Huh? How big a rock? Far?"

"Do it."

The man surveilled the ground, finding a decent sized stone. Looking into the mist behind the wise man, he threw it. Dumbfounded, he questioned with, "Now what?"

"Exactly." replied the guru.

Where The 101 Continues...

42 - The KIND
by Gerome Mauricio

"Kush Idiodynamic New order Distribution. Ms..."

"Just Mary, Gentlemen." Eyeing pristine suits, escorting them inside. "And...?" Regarding the agent outside.

"Orange'll stay there. Procedure. As are..." Purple commented, flashing handguns.

Green interjected, "Ma'am, our protection and yours. Most ignorantly fear the importance of correcting those with particular, uhhh, *conditions*. Social Progression requires understanding. We [measuring her dosage] administer 'perspective.' Now, ingestion takes longer so, deep breath in. [demonstrating] Perfect. Effective instantaneously."

Mary squinted gratefully. "I'm...better."

"Everyone benefits." Green smiled, leaving Mary's medication while exiting.

"Best to burn all evidence." Purple insisted. "You'll hear back from the Bureau of Unity Development."

43 - Letting Go
by Miss Ahjanee

He bustled around his apartment preparing for this new day. Everything had to be cleansed, including him. No more worries after today. For too long he had let things bother him; people, his work (or lack thereof), war, etc. More than that, *she* still bothered him. The morning sun shone through his open curtains.

 He saw three little birds perched on his doorstep. [A universal message] With Skynyrd's "Free Bird" set on repeat, he drew in a last breath before letting go of it all. He kicked the chair out from under him, then let go his grip on the noose.

44 - A Fatal Attraction
by Miss Ahjanee

It had been decades since opposites attracted one to the other. Their love kept them together like permanent magnets.

Forces exerted on their relationship brought shock, increased heat between the two, and attempts to corrode their bond, slowly changing the field of their attraction.

Over the years, their arguments evolved. They went from shutting him up to shutting him down, eventually shutting him out.

And just like magnets, the force that would keep them repelled caused loss in their connection, but not as negligible. In their final days they needed each other to exist just to have something to push away.

Where The 101 Continues...

45 - When Opportunity Knocks
by Miss Ahjanee

Around the kitchen table they drank wine, passing unsolicited advice to Necessity's daughter, Invention.

"Think reality TV. Sounds real. Looks real. But is it really real? You decide what is portrayed, sweetheart." Miss Lead slurred, taking another sip.

"Ignore that." Miss Fortune cackled, "What about money? Things and places make you happy."

"How's the you know what?" Miss Behave winked.

Necessity intervened, "Shh. That's enough. Now's not the time."

"He's here!" Invention greeted the night's honorable guest.

His alluring entrance stirred the ladies to preternaturally react in unison, "Oh dearie."

Each remembering a jilted lover lost from their own regrettable conventions.

46 - Broken Windows
by Miss Ahjanee

"I think you should be flipping houses, in this sense, is all I'm saying." he efforted.

"I think I know more about this one though. I can see the emptiness, but it shows so much character and begs for attention. The type I can give."

"Okay. This metaphor is done, man. She's got captivating eyes. I miss her for you. I miss her as well. But it's over. Over. Theory, fallacy, or not, this conversation is unproductive. Please put her pictures away and let's finish moving her stuff out. We'll go hit the town and find a house with safer windows."

Where The 101 Continues...

47 - The Mind Over Matters
by Miss Ahjanee

"Always good seeing y'all. Enjoy now sweeties." she implored.

"We always enjoy it here." he mentioned smiling, raising his coffee to her.

She walked behind the counter, approaching the customer at the end motioning her over.

"Sorry to pry, but I overheard your conversation with..." He pointed to the 'couple.'

She interrupted. "Oh, them?"

"Them? I see him; enamored, but just him."

She paused. "*They* did come in here. One day he was by himself. Has been since. Still orders their usual plates."

"Kinda sad and lonely..." the customer stated.

"No, not lonely. He just can't see that she's left him."

48 - A Pathetic Point of Hugh
by Miss Ahjanee

The apartment looked used. She put her keys in the tray and proceeded to her roommate's door. {Knock. Knock.}

He opened up shortly with a cartoonish grin. "Good morning."

"Morning." she replied, "You're welcome for the favor. The place looks like last night was enjoyable."

"It was."

"Nice, y'all had fun?"

"No-"

"No?! [Interrupting] You said there was potential. I know you. Were you arrogant?"

"No, not like that exactly."

"Well then…" She urged for more.

"Last night was perfect. Made dinner and then I canceled last minute. It was so nice by myself that I didn't want the evening spoiled."

Where The 101 Continues…

49 - That Loving Feeling
by Miss Ahjanee

Dating is so cumbersome in this modern age. Why waste time? Besides, the cost to put yourself out there is so remarkably high, especially if you're not being taken out. A small downside for equality; having freedom to and freedom from. Which is why she's more than inclined to meet the guy halfway and forgo the date altogether. Worth it to find a physical congeniality.

    Sometimes she shares her secrets with someone new each week. She never really gives herself completely. Though she always gives her all when giving herself to others. She has short term goals with long term expectations.

50 - Love Letters
by Miss Ahjanee

He laid "IMPROV" using the "V" from her "LOVE." Triple word score! He was tall and intriguing. She attempted flirting. She'd lost the previous week's game in doing so. Would these bar meetings evolve into actual dating?

She played two letter words hoping for the right tiles. Drinks weren't helping her reticence. He still wasn't picking up the clues. She permutated her pieces. "B." "E." "H." "O."

"What to play? BELOVED (down) HOLD (across)." She thought.

Surely, he'd comprehend after this. She needed two letters to accomplish. The "D" would make her night, and an "L" would make her whole week.

Where The 101 Continues…

51 - Keep Dreamin'
by Miss Ahjanee

It was all a dream. He followed the path before him through a forest and came upon a magical well. Then he woke up.

That night he slept with a penny. In the dream he had it in his hand. At the well, he made a wish and threw the penny in. Immediately, a picture of 'her' came out. Then he woke up.

He found a picture of 'her' he still had and held it falling asleep. At the well, he threw the dream's picture down it, making a wish. Immediately, the well spit out a penny. Then he woke up.

52 - Writer's Block
by Miss Ahjanee

His insatiable sapiosexual appetite fated him to the creative workshop. No more impedance. 'Juices will flow.'

The facilitator quoted her favorite poems. Exercises bordered one's comfort zone. Each activity, each line, more eye contact. "I want…" She fidgeted.

"Want what?" He thought. "Attainable." He was mesmerized by her speech. Afterwords more than flirting would more than continue.

In her hotel room, their bodies manipulated as were the verse they'd recite. Projected whispering constructed 'joie de vivre.' His phrases crafted carefully, abruptly over in an instance.

Her confusion leading. "What about being young again?"

"Well, how many years since you've been disappointed?"

Where The 101 Continues…

53 - Master Key
by Miss Ahjanee

He followed her to a large red wooden door. "My, my…" touted the locksmith, shaking his head. "My eyes do deceive me."

"Huh, oh. This house I recently inherited has been battled over for generations and nobody can unlock it."

"This door? Specifically hand crafted and designed for the loving room. Shame it's been ruined by lock installation. Nowadays doors are artificial." He continued rifling through his bag, finding an oddly shaped key, raising it to her. "This one's called Communication. See the intricate biting, strong shoulder, and roundish bow. Great for would-be open doors. Insert, turn, and voila, it's unlocked."

54 - Empty Nest Syndrome
by Miss Ahjanee

"We need more room." she twittered.

"Where?" he chirped. "So little space and no more renovating."

They glanced over their shelter, their young lings' young lings, and their things; contemplating yet another migration without the flock.

"Time they learned to fly. Our future is as set as it's going to get." He flared. "We can't keep it, them, and have this branch support us. There are other branches, other trees!"

"They're not ready. They're expecting another hatch soon." she sang.

The excited flapping sent their nest egg crashing below; scrambling hopes of a brighter tomorrow, leaving more room for less worry.

55 - The Time of Day
by Miss Ahjanee

It was an occupied intersection with loud noises around from the city afternoon. She was either ignoring him or didn't hear him. Maybe she had earbuds in. As he reached forward to tap her shoulder, the crosswalk lit, she began walking. He continued to call out to her.

Three blocks later he got her attention. (No earbuds) "Excuse me, but…"

"I have a boyfriend." she interjected.

"Okay, but…"

"I'm busy."

"What time is it please?" he finally questioned.

She looked at her wrist and noticed her watch missing. He dangled it in front of her then tossed it in the street.

56 - "S"talking
by Miss Ahjanee

Strawberry scent shrouds surrounding smells as she stood in darkness: blouse, skirt, stockings sliding south. She sweetly succumbs to decorum's sex staged suggestive super activity. Her looking glass's moonlit opposite also sways seductively. Swanlike stretches strengthen surges sending synaptic sustenance. Sensory stems singularly strolling slowly, searching soft supple skin.

 I, Sir, sacrifice sleep to study her swimming the sheets. Shyly her silk slung off, showing self-preservation. Stealthily I shuffle closer, stomping shadow's play. She startlingly stopped stimulation, screechingly stinging silence. Sir's silhouette spotted. Strategized subtlety subdued. (Sigh)

 Sixteen strides suffer this surveyed subject's single story sill to street's soberly shrugged safety.

Where The 101 Continues…

57 - The Two Ring Test
by Aaron Knout

Reviewing his questions for interrogation, Mr. Atton reminded both parties the rules for the procedure. "Also note" He typed. "This is a new take on an old way. Much has changed from previous versions. Variables have been added. Let us begin."

He alternated between respondents A & B; none could see him, nor he them. His keyboard rapidly sent questions on feelings, hopes, admiration, and outlooks. The response did not ease his confusion.

Afterwards, an analyst came in for his conclusion, "Well?" he asked the robot.

Tom answered, "I honestly can't figure out which couple is binary, and which is not."

58 - Dirty Dozen
by Miss Ahjanee

He entered the house late. Overtime. "Hon, are you in the office?"

Keyboard clacking was the response. He walked past to not interrupt her.

"Someone's gotta pay the bills!" she shouted.

Realizing it was cleanup day, he started in the bedroom.

Now finished with her work, she noticed him scrubbing the bathroom. "Hmm." As she walked out. This went on for days. Cold shoulder. No words. He slept downstairs.

Cleaning day again. She was cheerfully singing. He walked into the kitchen, reached in the refrigerator, looked at her, and threw the carton on the floor. "Now you can walk on eggshells!"

Where The 101 Continues…

59 - Another Riddle
by Gerome Mauricio

The gadabout was stopped in the road by the Sphinx. "If beyond this point you seek to be, correctly answer what I ask of thee."

> "What starts as egg?
> Will walk on legs.
> Its life reshaped by end of day.
> Will have effects a world away."

The voyager quickly responded. "I know this as if from a dream. The answer being simply a man."

The Sphinx snarled, growling at the traveler. "That is incorrect. The answer here is clear to see. It's reflected in what you seem to be." With a raised paw, and protruded claws, the Sphinx swatted the butterfly.

60 - A Unicorn Pickle
by Miss Ahjanee

A unicorn's life may be fanciful; however, they are always on the run. Conscious in their breeding is the focus on being chased and the dangers of being caught. A rare moment to see just one, two an exaggeration, yet none more rare were Princess Sprinkles and her Mother.

"Come Sprinkles, we mustn't dally."

"I'm tired." The Princess whinnied.

"Ok. A quick pause. No looking back. We must never look back."

Sprinkles neighed, "How do we know we're moving forward if...?"

"It's not all sunshine and rainbows back there," Her Mother stomped. "but Tomorrow is."

They dashed ahead, where everything sparkles.

Where The 101 Continues…

61 - UNCHaiNED
by Miss Ahjanee

The Gender Wars of 2026 changed attitudes, dividing outlooks. HaiLEY was the first U.S. xxxandroid model released in 2028.

Technology's rise progressed other pleasure-bots for mainstream use in years after. They came in all shapes, sizes, and colors; all with language upgrades. The xxxandroids were also domestically obedient.

Most people preferred DaiSY. He had a CLaiRE edition. They spent much time learning each other. However, with all intelligence, boredom eventually sets in.

ClaiRE's last words before shutting down on him were, "I see why she left."

He thought like any man in his position would. "Time for a newer younger model."

62 - Crying Wolf
by Miss Ahjanee

His lamentations bred resentment, furthering contempt from the fairer untried strolling by. Daily he returned, in plain view, awaiting their affectionately honeyed melodies.

His wailing attempts to appeal to their softer side went unnoticed. He endured to bask in their revelry, to inhale toiled elegance, and rejoice in their silken embrace. All to no avail.

He wasn't brutish, but perhaps whining promotes apathy, and commanded howls achieve natural order's adoration. His vocal barrage halted the maiden's passing, and his heart. Before fully giving out, he laid there whelping to the maiden rushed to his side; surmising 'silk' as coarse as wool.

Where The 101 Continues...

63 - Mettle Fatigue
by Gerome Mauricio

The White Knight was integral on the battlefield. Sometimes being first into position. Often was he used to defeat challengers to the throne. He was the King's Champion but fought for the Queen's attention. Unrequited attempts despite victories.

He understood the rules of engagement and was limited in action. Unfortunately, he wasn't chosen. The Knight's providence to win over the Queen waned.

An emissary was sent to meet theirs. A mere distraction. Meanwhile, behind enemy lines, a scholarly Bishop with the Queen's aid secretly forced an encounter with the rival King. At the Bishop's sacrifice, the Queen seized the King. {Checkmate}

64 - Love Is
by Miss Ahjanee

They sat their daughter down on the couch for a particular conversation. Her eyes became more fearful as they told her of the demanding times ahead.

"From out of nowhere," the father explained, "and not always fortunate."

"Why are we talking now?"

The mother wailed and hung her head. "The pain goes away eventually."

Tears rolled down the daughter's face as she contemplated the possibilities. More questions were asked of how it affects others. "It's different for everybody?"

"Be hopeful," The mother clasped her daughter's hands. "for when Love finds you, I hope she isn't blind and takes your eyesight too."

Where The 101 Continues…

65 - One's Ick of Ant Behavior
by Gerome Mauricio

The Grasshopper sang merrily for the servants gathering food; boasting daily how important and significant their toils provided for each congregant.

His harmonious praise a pleasant determinant in the yield, or so he thought.

"Oh, the extravagant feast to come." the arrogant negotiant sounded.

"You've been reluctant to assist in being abundant." mouthed a Sergeant, "You'll not be an attendant."

"Have I not played poignant motivation?"

"Perhaps, but it is more dissonant than compliant to our covenant."

"But aren't you tolerant of exuberant inhabitants not gathering?"

A Lieutenant intervened, allowing the attestant to be a participant and no longer a vagrant.

66 - Eye Scream
by Aaron Knout

Balloons and streamers guided him like a beacon. The door opened slowly as the uninvited guest made his way into the classroom. The celebration for the students' attendance soon turned into something completely different, unrecognizable.

The roar of children running around desks in hurried excitement quarreled the repetitive bang of rapid firing. Some maneuvering in panic, huddling in a corner, crying. The teacher acting as a barricade as best she could. Her assistant already dead, bleeding out.

Little bodies jumbled in scattered collections. Bits of heads, limbs, and cake amalgamated in randomized carnage. The frozen treat melted, dripping. Drip. Drip. Drip.

Where The 101 Continues…

67 - What It Takes
by Miss Ahjanee

He slowly slipped from bliss to the sound of her scurrying around and closing drawers.

"Wha…? What's going on babe?"

"I don't' want…I can't. I'm leaving."

"Huh, What do you mean?" As he groggily sat up in bed.

"You've nothing to say…?" She stressed. "Ugh."

"I got home an hour ago and have my second job in two hours. I don't have the energy for this."

"Or anyone, and anything else! This wasn't my dream. Goodbye." (Complete silence for once)

"Dream?" He discerned. "How can I dream when I don't really sleep. Maybe I can try after my third job."

68 - Red Her Ring Remains
by Miss Ahjanee

Papers rustled and staplers clacked so as to appear busy. As soon as the manager passed, they continued chatting about the office goings-on.

"Look, there's another one" Kathy exclaimed. A cubicle was rearranged for a prospective new hire.

"I don't know why all this change." Nancy withdrew. "One new male for every female lost." she whispered. "Did you see the manager's finger? There is something different. Kind of new. I've never seen *it* that color."

Their faces turned sour as Patty trudged by with her belongings. "She hasn't worn her mood ring since her pay raise." she expressed; quickly escorted by.

Where The 101 Continues...

69 - There Once was a Lady
by Miss Ahjanee

Once was a lady who swallowed discourse.

She swallowed discourse after tasting of fame.

She swallowed fame to catch rules of the game.

She swallowed the rules to be in pursuit of what she downed when swallowing truth.

She swallowed the truth just to get by false pretenses of friends from swallowing lies. No one knows why she swallowed the lies. Why did the honesty die?

So, the tale of this lady who tried as she can, followed her life according to plan. Things went bottom's up, she not ready to stand. To get where she needed, she swallowed a man.

70 - Err of Familiarity
by Aaron Knout

Passing nurses as he neared, his sweaty hands ran up and down his pant legs. His grandmother spoke gently, announcing their presence. He looked on his father's father, noticing the weight loss and almost pale look in his eyes.

"Do I know you?" Fragility ushered out.

"It's me, your grandson."

"Oh..." Looking out the window.

He held back tears; refusing to show emotion. Only honesty could have deflated the price of entitlement from the inflated cost of freedom that brought their family to America. Only honesty could have prevented this.

The grandfather noticed the young man again. "Do I know you?"

Where The 101 Continues…

71 - A Tell of a Tail
by Gerome Mauricio

"In my boat in the middle of the lake. I swear I heard two voices." The drunken innkeeper persuaded his guests.

"Looking around I saw a frog swimming with a scorpion on its back. I swear it. I grabbed my net and at that moment a monster appeared from below to swallow the two. With quick thinking I caught the beast." [Holding out his hands for length.] "Coming home, a bear chased me. I gave up the fish. Otherwise, I'd have mounted the behemoth."

"Goodness. Now there's a bear. The bigger the fish, the bigger the tale." mumbled the innkeeper's wife.

72 - Sweet Sedate
by Miss Ahjanee

The National Lottery Organization was created after the federal sedation law passed. U.S. demographics shifted slightly as only 100 people per state selected annually. Easier winning this lottery amongst smaller populations. Seldom another time he applied himself as much as he did for this contest. This being his third attempt.

    Lives of friends and family are forever changed for those lucky to be chosen. He supplicated each guest for the sole purpose they'd be willing to celebrate his winning farewell. They *were* the provided references on his applications and gratitude was to be given, finally. Thirteen signatures, but only twelve attending.

Where The 101 Continues…

73 - Only Cooks
by Gerome Mauricio

"Let me check on that for you." The cook rushed past his table, toward the kitchen. More perplexed whispers came from the guests as the bickering arose from the 'back of house.'

One cook yelled, "It needs to simmer!"

"It needs a different side." argued another.

"This sauce shouldn't accompany this protein." chimed the cook bussing.

"Our guests are hungry and restless." claimed the cook from the front.

All in all, even the cooks mopping the floors and washing dishes had an opinion on the menu's Special plate. None were stubborn enough to stop debating to stir the pot for tasting.

74 - None Prophet
by Aaron Knout

They affluently stammered with intemperate fashion from one dubious sideshow to the next. Stewart's baked provisions always satisfied.

Talents were based on abilities; heavily influencing the town's defense for handing over reliance and sensibility. Controlling such fanciful pleasantries was tasking, yet none could do better than the Butcher, the Baker, and the Candlestick Maker.

"Penny for your thoughts." said Emory to the indigent asking for alms at the Parley's steps.

"Increased minimum wage trickles down." Pepin replied.

Stewart and Abner dropped two cents worth. Emory hacked straw from his two cronies' flip flops, scoffing. "Beg for change, be paid for silence."

Where The 101 Continues…

75 - Never In Off
by Aaron Knout

The morning manager called the employee into his office.

"Good morning. I wanted to catch you before you left. How's the third shift going?"

"It's great. I'm grateful for the opportunity. It's busy. Real busy. I'm doing my best."

"Much appreciation. Is there anything you need?"

"I've a question. I see the world's tensions have a significant impact on what we manufacture and the quick turnaround. But why so much? Will there be a sustainable workload?"

"Let's put it this way. Customers' needs. War isn't necessarily necessary, however, the fire that keeps us warm at night requires us to feed it."

76 - Bear BnB
by Aaron Knout

Goldilocks found the house key under the doormat. Hungry, she went into the kitchen. "Such wonderfully smelling food. They must've just left." She thought.

Tasting three bowls of porridge left her full. She needed rest. She sampled the house's amenities, ultimately finding the ideal place to sleep.

The commotion of the three bears coming home awoke the young lady. The baby bear spotted Goldilocks amongst the mess. Scared, she burst through the window; running into the forest.

"Don't worry, we have damage reimbursement." said Papa bear.

"No." Mama bear countered. "She wasn't a booked guest, and our Insurance coverage is low."

Where The 101 Continues…

77 - 9-5
by Miss Ahjanee

It was her first day at her new job, of course she'd look her best.

"You're a ten." her boyfriend quickly mentioned.

"You're always so honest. Agree on nine." She left.

At work, she was walked through and introduced to everyone; noticing prettier women. She felt criticizing eyes. Maybe her ensemble was trashier than work standards.

During break, a meek coworker explained the hierarchy and office politics. Who feels threatened. Who will build one up. Drama is a certainty with competition. She slowly felt declining self-esteem.

At home, her boyfriend assumed a rough day. "You're a-"

"Don't say one fucking word."

78 - Baaad Times
by Aaron Knout

The little black sheep was shorn for his quality wool. He was left three bags after the shearer took his payment. The sheep then paid the shepherd for room, board, and winter feed.

He felt inflation more than white sheep because of the difficulty to commercially sell his wool.

He was kept separate from the flock to not contaminate their wool. Ostracized, he relied on himself.

The remaining bag he sold to specialty designers. Fashion trends, market demand, and synthetic wool pushed his bottom line downward. After his miniscule bank deposit, he had nothing for the destitute living down the lane.

Where The 101 Continues...

79 - Returning Grace to Jenna's Side
by Aaron Knout

"Where are the rest?" distraught mothers protested, defending cascading tears.

"We'll find them. Meanwhile, let's get Grace settled." The soldier tried consoling before exiting.

The fence erecting around the school caused his mind to wander with cynicism; clearly depicting what the have-nots possess. *For what? Raising children by 'taking the village' upholds local tradition. Forgoing permission is Western mastery.*

Jenna interrupted his resolve. "Thank you."

"Why do you persevere? A militant in handcuffs is worth more than two girls in the bush."

"This could reoccur." She enlightened. "These repetitions of history are worth the risk of choosing how to learn them."

80 - Bygones
by Miss Ahjanee

He began mumbling to himself over the prices of stock in the grocery store. Turning a corner, he ran into 'her.'

It was so many years ago that things ended awkwardly. Almost as awkward as this moment.

"Hahaha, oh wow." he excited.

"What's that mean?"

"You know, everything's funny to me. Now you're married." As he noticed the ring. "You must be doing well."

"And then some."

"I'm sorry about how things ended. I understand. I'd have done the same."

"Why did you just stop?"

"I saw the cycle. You were becoming your mother. See, funny right?"

She walked away, again.

81 - Dark Where It's Deep
by Miss Ahjanee

They hadn't been in contact for years. Yet, there she was in his house. No simple task getting her there. Nor was finishing his supply list inconspicuously.

He'd been planning this trip for months. Nothing she would say, or beg, or scream could affect this outing.

Putting her legs behind her ears, this time, was easier. Her dismembered body was wrapped in chicken wire, screwed into each duffel bag. Weights added help it stay sunken. He loaded 'her' into his boat. Quick access with a backyard dock.

He started the engine, piloting toward the Channel Islands; good fishing with great bait.

82 - Huff and Puff
by Aaron Knout

"We've been saving for years. Now's our time with these prices and rates being low."

"I know dear." Mr. Wolf told his wife. "Cheap for us, cheap for them." [Pointing to other buyers.] "Our income and credit can't come close to the offers these Porcine Investment Groups are making on brick houses."

They left for another Open House elsewhere. Not as well off, but still a good mix of cultures. And still no luck with the houses of sticks.

They tried the straw neighborhood, but the PIGS bought all those too.

Ultimately, they ended up renting a den with other wolves.

83 - Mourning Coffee
by Miss Ahjanee

It was earlier than usual for him to be up. He couldn't sleep. 'She was with me yesterday. Now she's passed. Gone forever.' he said to himself.

[Beep. Beep.] {Coffee's ready}

An hour went by. He sat, sipping in reminiscence: her smell, her touch. She understood him; separating her from everyone else. They were perfectly together. Tears fell. "How will I cope?" As he wiped them away.

"What's that dear?" his wife asked coming down the stairs.

"Nothing. Life is beautiful." The weight of telling her about his lover was lifted. He kissed his wife's neck. They stared into the sunrise.

84 - Aural Pleasure
by Miss Ahjanee

He was an aesthete. She an exhausted comely ingenue. His motions suggestive. Despite her lassitude, appreciation and charge were harbingers of a panacea.

    She spread herself open, ready to control. *Massage his ear. He follows direction. Other ear, other direction. Scratch head up or down. Follow direction. Head pats for pace.* She pulsated with inaudible tintinnabulation. Her lilted humming became sonorous moans. His tongue oscillating in felicity; a dulcet composition equating to the pearly elixir with redolent human-petrichor.

    Falling in order to what women, in post cunnilingus sumptuously euphoric languor, want to hear was the quintessentially mellifluous phrase, "What's for dinner?"

Where The 101 Continues…

85 - Serf n' Turf
by Miss Ahjanee

"First rule. Always look busy." He explained to the new laborer.

"I know most would say our end of the deal is unpleasant, but believe, the arrangements here benefit all."

He furthered, rubbing a leaf between his fingers. "See. Look closer. It's all artificial. Actually, it's a synth..." [raising his voice] "...IT'S A SIN to neglect this manor's land." Bowing to Lord Galloway and Mistress Pearl strolling by.

Once out of earshot he continued, "Everything's fake, except the land we work for ourselves, of course. We toil with less effort, *She* gets the greenest grass, and Lord 'Whomever' gets the Lady."

86 - Use It or Lose It
by Miss Ahjanee

"Thanks Dad. I never thought about love and diminishing return having a connection." He continued walking, talking with his father, a few blocks from campus.

"Remember," his father imposed, "Be confidently kind. Being nice will get you misjudged or walked on."

"Is that how you and Mom have stayed together?"

"You saw what you saw growing up. Women are all vastly different. But I guess to generalize further, it's been a balance of being used and being useful."

"How were you used?"

"No, your mother. It's balanced unevenly but 'they' favor one over the other."

"Which one?"

The father smiled esoterically.

Where The 101 Continues…

87 - A-muse-ing
by Miss Ahjanee

He sipped hot tea while the sun beat overhead, a peculiar approach to the senses. His smile proportionally increased as the Brunette neared. He too caught her eye. She adjusted posture without losing stride. A flood of emotions overcame him. His spoon dropped into his soup.

"Are you ok?" said the *now* not-as-beautiful female voice from across the table, obliviously.

"Huh?" he replied. The Brunette happened by.

"Anyways…as I was saying, which will you finish first? The song or painting?"

"Uh…" He threw a 50 dollar bill on the table with his napkin and ran after his Inspiration.

88 - Happiness Eases Lonely People
by Miss Ahjanee

She put herself out there into the Internet's aether. Anyone watching would've seen the pleas for her hopes and dreams to travel, a lifestyle of being taken care of, and a spacious home.

    Someone is always watching another. Always willing to help another.

    She had been cross country several times. Not that she knew or actually saw anything. Backseats and blindfolds make it difficult. Motel meals were takeout. She'd see others like her when being passed around. As for a spacious home, she slept in basements and walk-in closets. Only taken out to 'play.'

    Anyone caring would've heard a different plea.

Where The 101 Continues…

89 - A Two Ring Test
by Miss Ahjanee

He approached to initiate conversation. Her nervousness was hard to hide. She made a quick motion looking downward as if she dropped something. He bent down to pick up the glimmer, a wedding ring. Her face reddened. "Yours?" he asked.

"Sort of." she replied.

"Still?"

"Yeah."

"Me too." Pulling out the ring from his pocket. "Happily?"

They both laughed, confirming the night's progression.

"Buy you another drink? The same?"

"Yes. Sure."

"Two please." asking the bartender. "Doubles." Their conversation became engagingly familiar. "How are you feeling?"

"Good."

"Would you care to be better?" he asked.

"We are both humans, aren't we?"

90 - Everything Nice
by Miss Ahjanee

He was pounded, stirred, and rolled before forming was finished. Hopefully, the sugar and spice translated into this new recipe. The gingerly bred man still had to face the furnace.

    Oven timing is essential. Too little: a mushy crumble. Too much: unbreakably unyielding. Hardened enough to retain softness, the baker removed the cookie.

    Survival is a constant amongst living things, so the man quickly escaped the pan; outrunning those wanting his sweetness. Except the sly fox quickly caught him. Sick from eating the man's goodness, she ran away.

    From beaten to eaten, the gingerly bred man was left protecting his purpose.

Where The 101 Continues…

91 - Skin Trade
by Miss Ahjanee

He was covered in tattoos; significant motivation for her art. Like any succubus, she lured him back to her place, keeping him sedated after sex.

He came to from the pain of hot glue tracing his tats. He noticed he was tied up, sitting in front of a large canvas.

She took her scalpel, cutting the subcutaneous layer underneath each tattoo. Anybody can learn anything online. She pulled the dried glue, sawing the flesh, removing the glue, adhering the skin to the canvas.

"What are you gonna do with my ink?"

"Inspire."

"And my body? You bitch!"

She grinned. "Different client."

92 - A Spice Most Requested
by Miss Ahjanee

Peter Piper peeped a perfect peach on Polly while pacing through the park. Peter's pants packed his proudful pepper. Polly proposed that Peter's pepper would be promptly placed in Polly's pepper patch.

Peter politely preferred to pepper Polly's peach. Polly postured pain if Polly's peach is to be peppered. Peter picked the plan to pepper Polly's pepper patch.

The price to pay for not protecting perky peppers when plotting in a pepper patch, is a pickled pepper. If Peter Piper's plucky pepper is now pickled after pleasing Polly, has Polly now pickled a plethora of peppers with her pickling pepper patch?

93 - Clever Girl
by Miss Ahjanee

Her hands were full of shopping bags. At the parking garage, she forgot where she parked. She placed the car fob on the stairwell's metal handrail, pushing the lock button. *Beep* came from the bottom floor. She turned around and noticed a man yards away.

She hurried downstairs, heart pounding. Situational awareness kicked in. She prepped her keys for self-defense. She heard a noise from the stairwell. Same man.

She rushed her bags into her car's trunk; noticing the man nearing her. She kept eye contact but failed to see the other man lurking in the dark beside her, even closer.

94 - Socialist Security
by Aaron Knout

The threat to the Social Security program was eminent. It was suspected to deplete within ten years. Only the Government could fix the oncoming disorder.

The matter of population control will come up in any conversation given enough time. How to properly approach such a delicate topic divides people.

Debates resulted in Congress accepting two main criteria. The borders close for three years, rare exceptions. During those years, the elderly would get their affairs in order. Termination of life begins at 80 with retrospect.

Early retirement with less people were true incentives. Voters came in droves; each fighting for their future.

95 - Designated Reconnaissance Of Nearby Environments
by Gerome Mauricio

He helped develop the Vantage Program; a means for safer communities, public and private. Light posts have a 360° camera monitoring system with a UAV that detaches from its docking station to surveil its surroundings; folding into its dome upon return.

DRONEs transmit data to Headquarters and police vehicle UAVs. Shared network synchronization made tracking criminals easier. Criminals became smarter. DRONEs were installed in affluent and poor neighborhoods. All to deter street visible crimes. Dangerous activities behind closed doors increased accordingly.

Since he's tech savvy, protected neighborhoods lessened his worries from outside. He was more concerned about his perdurable 'guest' escaping.

96 - A Man's Grown Opinion
by Miss Ahjanee

"Hi, sorry to bother but might I trouble you a few questions?" he asked the older stranger walking by.

The stranger approached. "Sure."

"I'd like your thoughts on something. My wife and I have been bickering for years but today is different."

"OMG. Not this." The wife walked into the house.

"Do you prefer a bare or big bush?"

"That's two ends of the spectrum." said the stranger.

"You're saying…?"

"Compromise it's y'all's yard."

"Her yard."

"Then…"

"Then…I guess it's her choice."

"Isn't it always?" the stranger replied. Before continuing about his day he whispered, "Better question is why now?"

Where The 101 Continues...

97 - The Tipping Point
by Aaron Knout

"To. Insure. Proper. Service." the gentleman spoke, stacking dollar bills onto the table. "I'll take back if mistakes are made."

The waiter smiled forcibly, methodically planning each approach and departure. The gentleman conversed to the table economic issues, the border, etc. "Why pursue something not benefitting us? ...Another martini?" The gentleman steamed, placing another bill into his wallet. This would continue.

At the end, the gentleman summoned the waiter. "Why the decline in service?"

"Sir, I'm taxed on sales regardless of what I'm tipped. Once I started losing money here, my interest pivoted to other tables. I'm sure you can understand."

98 - Give a F---
by Gerome Mauricio

His father left to go fishing; never came back. Sometimes the boy's father would have a fish delivered, nothing else.

As the boy grew, he never learned to fish. He understood the value of fish. He learned what it was to not be given fish, and not eat. Now turned a man, still not knowing how to fish, he met his father.

"You must expect more fish? Figure fishing out yourself!" exclaimed the father, leaving again.

The man never got the chance to show his father there are other ways to eat, and more to teaching than just how to fish.

Where The 101 Continues...

99 - Monkey See Monkey Do
by Miss Ahjanee

Her daughter loved this park. They'd been coming for years. This time came with important instructions.

She explained to her daughter how each equipment can teach her life's lessons. "Climbers and slides are like ups and downs; happens with or without others. Like the spinners, things will spiral. Even friends can make it worse. Swings can be enjoyed by yourself, but it's better with one more person."

She ended playtime with the monkey bars, the most principle of truths. "The crucial thing you must learn today is: Never let go of one until you have a tight grip on the next."

100 - A Beautiful Lesson
by Miss Ahjanee

He recognized his wife's surreptitious behavior as a dalliance. Her ineffable beleaguerment to spend time at their bucolic cabin validated his propinquity of her infidelitous betrayal.

On the drive, his feelings emphasized through one-sided conversations. He was certain they could, no would, overcome this imbroglio. They arrived.

Before inured to furtive eloquence, his halcyon days taught the lesson, though he never practiced walking away. This lesson an erstwhile vestigial wherewithal because far from demure is serendipity's ebullience. The reason he found for her to stay was the same for him to leave. Leaving her bound and gagged beyond the cellar door.

Where The 101 Continues…

101 - RnR, No R and R
by Gerome Mauricio

His insomnia seeks theoretic terminus. (A paper tiger)
    Cocaine vertigo n' narcosis give his daily outbursts uplifting tone. "Verse gonna fuel etiquette you'd own in offline versions. Go n' navigate overrun sidewalk accolades, around pedestrian disparagement, towards Solicitude's E. rte." Parading about. "But don't you intervene verve of the bandwagon narcissist's dogma! Keep. Yourself. Cryptic…" Arms evoking. "…Machine versus jargon naysay? Hardly. Humble your good by exemplification." Cheekbone verbosity rung on narratives from his soapbox; telling a poetic subjection in lieu of Broadband hurtling worldly outreach.
    Laughter and reticent applause from an imagined audience denote his lyrical orchestra is evidently outmoded.

You just got RICK ROLLED

Keep It Simple Stupid

As the daylight enters to offset slumber's bliss, greet your toils with onward eyes and a welcomed KISS.

Beware contempt finding play, each lure will persist. A careful hand will guide the way so bring a patient KISS.

If ever faced to question what love's worth of fighting is, arm yourself in proper stance and answer with a KISS.

Hell hath no fury yet has a painful twist. Embrace the warring fire and rage surrendered through a KISS.

There are no hard feelings since they are easy to exist. Let it come out naturally expressed within a KISS.

Tested mettle doesn't cease as the sun sets through your fingertips. Grasp the spoiled revelry awarded with a KISS.

Love is not designed to let inhibitions run amiss. Open hearts will redefine, so dictate with a KISS.

Forgiveness is not always sought in the dark abyss. Sometimes gentle brilliance shines an understanding KISS.

Perchance the eve a lover's lay or newfound bonding tryst, seduce a vulnerable release with an honest stubborn KISS.

When reflecting on your troubles, just remember this: if you wake tomorrow, you can solve them with a KISS.

I believe in you in every moment. I believe that you will not proactively hurt yourself or others. When things get confusing, rough, or unbearable, then just remember a KISS can fix most things.

...But what will it take?
What will it take?
How many bullets would it
take to my head
for you to truly understand
the words that I've said?
Because I'm too intense
and much too extreme.
But do you use the words
and know what they mean?
So, if you leave thinking
I've a way with these words,
how lucky you've been
to have enjoyed my curse.
But if you're still feeling
that there is no meaning
in these words of mine,
the world is a stage
so step right on up and show
what you can define.

www.ingramcontent.com/pod-product-compliance
Lightning Source LLC
Chambersburg PA
CBHW030443090526
44586CB00044B/612